JANUARY MACHINE

Also by Rob Schlegel

The Lesser Fields

JANUARY MACHINE

Rob Schlegel

Four Way Books
Tribeca

Please direct all inquiries to:
Editorial Office
Four Way Books
POB 535, Village Station
New York, NY 10014
www.fourwaybooks.com

Library of Congress Cataloging-in-Publication Data

Schlegel, Rob.
[Poems. Selections]
January machine / Rob Schlegel.
pages cm
ISBN 978-1-935536-44-4 (alk. paper)
I. Title.
PS3619.C424J36 2014
811'.6--dc23

2013036097

This book is manufactured in the United States of America and printed on acid-free paper.

Four Way Books is a not-for-profit literary press. We are grateful for the assistance
we receive from individual donors, public arts agencies, and private foundations.

NATIONAL
ENDOWMENT
FOR THE ARTS

This publication is made possible with public funds from the National Endowment for the Arts.

[clmp]

We are a proud member
of the Council of Literary Magazines and Presses.

Distributed by University Press of New England
One Court Street, Lebanon, NH 03766

CONTENTS

for Brandon Shimoda

Bellwethers

I have in mind the way the mind recalls painful moments more sharply than pleasurable ones, or the way stories about stable, successful protagonists bore pretty much everyone. It's not a matter of developing a capacity for existing in such contradictions, as if you could master and harness those traumas "for the powers of good" but just that they are. They're like other beings living among us. You might deny they exist, and avoid them for a while, but eventually you're going to walk right into one.

Brent Cunningham

I was just writing to say that beth and I are down in browning and that because we have no computer access we are not sure how to do the constructive criticism. We are worried bc we want to do it right but right now we're broke and stranded. We might be heading back on Friday to sell paintings so we can get a little gas money to bring our car and kid back down. I just wanted to inform u of our situation. I know it sounds strange but I swear this Is the truth.

email from a former student

Among other forms and subjects, no subjects, landlord political sex suppressed, tied only with categories of experimental workouts, poems for the dead and I don't know.

Bernadette Mayer

I'm writing to keep u up to par with our situation—we didn't make it to Missoula b/c we got in a big fight and separated for a good while. We just reconciled and decided that dropping this course isn't the smartest thing to do. We're looking for a ride back to Missoula to get our clothes and books and other stuff. Rob, I want to be honest with u. This 4 day trip has turned into a complete nightmare I feel like giving up on everything. Maybe our car breaking down was a sign that we shouldn't have left. We want to keep in this because writing may be the only thing that gets us by. We have no money, no house no resources like relatives to help us. Our only opportunity is a job at the prison in Shelby.

email from a former student

This is what I like about the world. It just keeps asking, Here is another aspect. Do you see it? Are you listening?

Will Eno

No matter the thought or value, the poem will be bad, to make a pigeon roar.

William Carlos Williams

When it rings, the phone is a violence
but Youna's voice is a dozen
birds, and through the receiver
I can hear the president talking

until his voice is drowned out
by the dog barking down the street,
which suddenly seems
just like the street in that previous city

where all of this started on the back
of a motel receipt totaling $48.52
for a view of The Outback

and three men pissing from a fire escape
after ringing in the New Year
beating a gay couple with pieces of 2x4

leftover from a jobsite in Nashville,
Tennessee, where families
under pressure listened to music
celebrating the genders

and I was somewhere
in the middle, pretending to be
in touch with the state of the union.
Relying on cops and pedestrians

high on Monster, I helped a man
tie a mattress to the roof of his car
as he prepared for a month at the rehab center

where residents claim that after we die
we will all be carried off in paper canoes
drifting down the flooded avenues.

:::::::

Medium-sized American eyes.
Medium-sized American attention.
I am an American television
pipe bomb. Medium-sized

American fear. I am an American
television commercial. I exhibit
unusual. I am an American
unusual behavior. I exhibit

an overture, local—to what—to use
and useful. Limit of language,
limit of mind. Let national

be the sound of apples growing,
yellow salsify, opening and closing,
I am the I undone, immersed

in perspective, medium-sized
American diamond. Medium-sized
American pear. From the chimney,
I am smoke blown sideways.

Saint Ice, Saint Anthony,
Saint Destruction, find for me
a water deep enough to drown
these straws of indifference.

I am an American sigh, a limit
of language, a limit of privilege,
in this excess, a thousand exits

though none named Rosenbaum
who was wont to say: I want blues singers,
not just singers of blues songs.

Around those whose agendas
are national, I need to know
what national is. Its use seems limited
to the human condition,
but its condition seems fueled
by privilege. Providing a continent
with names—historical,
formal, or otherwise—gives it boundaries,
but it's the size of the country
that overwhelms me. In each moment
of silence a new consciousness.
I want again that feeling of being
engaged in the world—into language
I am putting back my body.

Here I am sipping 36 ounces of Coke
from tiny plastic straws
and wondering what the Japanese
are calling the ocean these days.
I give my order to the server
who says her face was lifted by a surgeon
admired for his spontaneity.
The man at the table next to me
can't hear his hearing aid battery beeping.
The T.V. news comes and goes
in grips of laughter, then tears.
Tonight, there is a little uncertainty in everyone—
the party of two sits at a table for a party of four
and the party of six is tipping.

Meanwhile, the state of Tennessee
is bracing for a freeze and I am coming
to terms with the fact that
some of this is written out of need,

the rest out of fear, or forgiveness,
which I sometimes hear in streets
I walk at night listening to families
recalibrate their moods to the various

tones of human speech and the birds
are looking for places to glimpse
their own reflections so that when

they despair they might feel witnessed,
as I do when I glance into a lit window
and see a man staring into the blankness

of his living-room wall and the privacy
within my head is suddenly less
private as he turns his face and locks
his eyes in mine, which startles me,

so I begin to hum, as if joining
the choir's final song, and just then
he invites me in, removes my clothes
and covers my body with green

paint before pressing me against
the wall. Once we are gone,
he says, this will prove we became

something more than who we are.
Outside his house, the flowers
grow bleak in the garden's dim bloom

and the tune I began is still
going on, and as the paint dries fast
the tune continues and the green
diminishes and the living-room wall

reveals evidence of our insistence
and the clarity of my thinking
leaves with the season and the radio
airs a marathon of threats—

as if these birds are holy because
their wings match the color of blossoms
caught in the morning light,

as if these birds are holy
because their bones fill with the same air
into which they fall in order to fly.

:::::::

I wish to stow this one perspective
in a house, and torch it.
Tell me again the contours
of this affliction, its horizon,

vertical as if it too were lying down
with its eyes open till its mind
were as receptive as I am
when I'm falling asleep, not myself

but a we trying to say what the I
might otherwise feign. Only when I'm alone
can I see my true nature—

how to express it through suppression,
cinnamon toast; slices of orange
—each morning is the memory

of my mother's breath, the smell of her
saliva thumbed across my face
to clean it. She used to watch me watch
my snow-people melt in the sun.

Did I know what death meant then?
Do I now? and what
does it mean, walking the streets
of the city, I become the city,

but those people in the choppers
are watching. Local, I know the houses,
the people who think paranoia

is a kind of flower a thinking
goes in and a thinking comes out
and I can tell by my voice

I am thinking of others and I know
that nothing is free and I can tell
by my nerves I am losing my way
in these lines of convoluted

thinking—for you, I have made a music
—I have me, I have me, I have me,
this hour and the next
and a damaged thing cannot

resist what damaged it. When eating
ash is considered a disease
what have we come to know

of the difficulty to remain one person
in this line of pushcarts pulled
through whose parade but ours?

So far from any song that might
save them, birds build
nests out of fear and fruit.
In the city, everyone continues
to do what they do. A few problems
are solved by talking, the rest
are folded into paper airplanes
and launched toward a smaller
economy. Am I of the salt,
or eating it? By its storage
I partake in the commerce of prediction—
an offer of lilacs where vespers
are products of stillness and ivy
is penitence tethered back.

::::::::

Restless smell of water, smell
of algae, a growing smell
and a sudden change in water
levels. I cannot register

the new medium, its slight
change in temperature. The city
is choked with celebrities.
I fail to recognize the movements

of lekking birds, trade of goods
between hill families—cannibals
comparing notes—sun in thighs,

in bowels. One mother lures
Surgeon's Astronomy
from obscurity into profit.

The cats are eating the calm.
Grief makes a sound like a toy
trumpet blown into a tiny room—
suppose the wind could carry

the sound of it—insane
wind at the corner of Front
and Main where a man stands
partly contained within a cage

of lath mudded with plaster.
He calls it a house to hold
his love, a house to hold

the corpses, a house to hold
the ashes. He calls it a house to hold
animals tethered to rafts

and sent downstream. A house
to hold the sun, a house to hold
the people looking forward
to spring but the people looking forward

to spring are the people
looking forward to their own
deaths, so he calls it a house to hold
the children, but the children

are heirs to the illness,
so he calls it a house to hold his rage,
but his rage is being watched

so he keeps thinking of new names
and the country is casting off its skin
and it looks like growing people.

Hysteria's hands reach so far.
The climates are planning a coup
with the ghosts of shot birds
whose meat is boiled from bone—
its marrows of height—an overture
long overdue. Wind comes and goes
across the soft faces of young
men slipping glimpses;
young women not pushing strollers
are watching the women who are.
In the grocery line, people
whose postures imply every apology
for proximity. Such splendid
little wars we forgive each other for.

:::::::

I carve the apple into the shape of a pear,
the pear into the shape of its seed
but it's the yellow rub of squash blossom
against my thigh that teaches me

how to behave in the siege of wings—
each minute some crow screaming at its kin—
fervor, favor—the seat on the boat
I exit before falling victim to seizures

afflicting birds turning the sky
into a tapestry of sound. On dry land I lift
the soil to my face as a way of singing

its praise and wind moves the trees
from which I pull a dozen leaves to offer
the crows in hopes of calming their panic.

I sit on the ground imitating a pear
rotting into grass, a pear I was not there
to catch and I cannot help
but take the blame for that so I check them

for bruises and stare at the people
who stare at me and I can tell
by the way they have rolled up their sleeves
they've not spent enough time

around water, and a crow lights on the roof
of the house to settle the dervish of birds,
and a crow lights in the tree of slaughter

and my hands bruise the meat of the fruit
as the grass is littered with feathers—
phrase and fable, my impossible failure—

Hysteric Variation

A white shirt falls from the sky

its arms move
like nothing I have ever seen

I scare birds off shore
by moving my jaw up and down
as shapes of bodies vary

Pale spires cast shadows of regular
length over the sacred
ground I live nearby

I look out over the water

There is a posture there
and I recognize it

From a distance the horizon is a place
and so is the mind

•

Faces take names for neon
fruit extending safety

into glass colonies

sincere as my attempt to speak
on behalf of my faith in me

I filter grief through notes
gendered mouths cannot release

Out of choice

Out of love

What progress means to nation

•

Heeding warnings form reveals
lines relieving pressure
trapped beneath
doors floating on the sea

I live in fear till fear becomes
that part of me
impossible to face

:::::::

Theaters of mollusk surrender props
wind tosses against this house
where I sit washing salt off my face
without coral, without towers

I can hear the sea narrating rumors
from middle America
where the high grass does not mark
the edge of the beach, nor the shorebird's

absence returned as stress between
genders in the losing half of
April when fear is a venue in states,

in cities beneath silent skies crazed
with clouds manmade by men
who resemble me listening for snow,

representing Plan B to find three
heads talking past each other
in the January machine, faster now
that it's focusing pain in strays eating

yellowcake in alleys. Nothing I say
is straight. The seahorses make paths
inside me. Of course it will hurt to die.
Trending life for libel anxiety burns

body to body, like a virus, but minor
and hardly recognizable in the last house
on the left where the poem is unreal

but I'm in it with ministers in clothes
granting access to patrons
in search of the west. I leave to be quiet

as figures in windows, in patterns
of birds in the park a man
rests his hand on the breast of a statue
and pulls out his phone to take

what is left of the calm with his finger
and I stop making sense after five
days of silence in porn without saints
my voice without speaking is a text

without volume, but no one is listening
as medias breathe through walls
by the second I fall into fiction when

no one is watching, I leave a few pills
for the faces not sleeping in halls
with disorders, kids and their genders

—it's all about you, it's all about me
doing my best to keep them from cutting
or worse on the street where I'm staring
at planes tearing the sky with steady explosions

as parts of the body part with the body,
and the only question love indwells
is left for the flowers pressing cement,
marking the limbs of the missing thou

stuffing blossoms into our ears
till we begin to hear what the dying hear
and strip our teeth to music made by pigeons

flushed from three pianos as earth
shrugs off its shawl of dirt and the fists of spring
bruise the buds a velveter black.

What Is Most Important from One Generation to the Next

The novel is too much in a mass culture,
The poem is too little. I feel a near

Paralyzing anxiety to speak if speaking
Means I will repeat myself.

I try to change the message before
the message changes me into a freedom
machine transforming fear into glee,
but the yellow bird's yellow wing
is caught between the wiper
and the windshield and the all-time greats
are on the verge of taking action.
I scramble for another way to see
the flag before eagles circle
overhead like kids gathering around
something dead in the park
where cocks branch off in peculiar stances
behind plastic structures which is where
my fear of heroes somehow starts.

Static

Thrust and Ache

Someone's phone rings in the coffee shop.
A man reading the paper says, "Cardinal."

A woman silences the phone. "It is a cardinal,"
The man says. "It is not," the woman says.

:::::::

Breathing through a little
anxiety, I'm thinking how nice
it would be to go back
to writing quiet poems with leaves

and trees and rocks from early
family vacations when waves arrived
with digital precision
and the ocean was blue and beautiful

and no one cared what it meant
to be national and listening
to the Brassens compositions

was passivity in notes disappearing
in the sea's authorial waves
and mirrors on the beach

were violent repairs—formal ideals
in movements, in curtains,
in hands to the face, and suspense
was a vessel of false relief in cold

air outside love change and awkward
capital in starts and stops
pressing the sky the Realists wished
to fill with nests torched

from trees dark with limbs beneath
snow looking down the mind.
But mind is this much control

and stable as it is, it is ever
a stranger talking, less alive but faster
each year tracking aggressive

love time when everything
around me is mythic in updates
borrowed from others
and I am at least as approachable

as Alan at the party Blake left
for drawing and inside the building
I can feel the building sway
as my attempt to light a match

attracts officials thinking terror
and No Robbie is a title
that won't stick, like snow on April

pavement, or narratives made up
as I go, like life or mind spilling
over as more or less poetry.

Static

Counting Picnics Between Phrases

The birds open and close their
Lovely wings. Is standing paralyzed

And staring into the bathroom
Mirror also a form of life?

:::::::

Stoned on the calming vibration
of the phone in my pocket, I step
out of the last house in Brooklyn
and cross on the ferry to Joe's Shanghai

where I'm learning to be alone
by watching other people. In Midtown
a man jumps from a window.
In Midtown sounds naked yet authorial.

If life is more or less predetermined
by days and weeks crumbling like sandstone
in fake waterfalls, then here I am

and here I'll be at least until the craze
dies down. One hundred, ninety-three,
eighty-six unremarkable ways to be afraid.

I see my face in the faces of others
exiting the subway, staring at necklines,
hoping some semblance of order
might reveal itself, I watch the sky

for stars falling. Someone puts a hand
beneath my chin and turns my face
to the left to see the Haitians on
the jumbo-cam. I check the temperature

of the fountain and construct my palaces
of reaction, but its not how I
envisioned it ending. With my boot-soles

on the ground, there is already enough
somewhere blossoming into separate
oceans and the popular singer is blushing.

Static

On the Bus

A woman whispers into her hands, quietly,
Then with a little violence. By the time

My life is spent the seats are empty
Part of the way, and mostly beige in color.

:::::::

Youna says she is quitting her job
because her boyfriend's band
is finally getting big. She tells me
to cut my books into paper children

and hold their hands while crossing
the street. I should hire a sitter
who can play a little music,
then visit a place I will never forget.

I'm driving 80 with sweaty bangs
and listening to movie stars
discuss glossy scenes elected

officials refuse to watch because
they are too busy updating The Fighting
Kits. I drive off the road till paranoia

spreads like prairie-fire toward
the abandoned school. Green with ivy
and other greenery, I run like a cop
through fields ruined with thinking.

Relationship to mind has changed.
I love the swans on the fences and these
oranges are sweeter than those
I pulled from the fire Youna started

before she cleaned the road kill
deer in the sea. Hers was
a house of crows finishing cats,

three days dead. And it's true
that we cried, then went outside
and stood very still in the night,

and it's true that the moon
broke through the roof and failed
to resemble the moon, and being no moon
was eventually gifted for swans

long staring into the faces of those
whose lives make little sense
beyond prescriptions to relieve
that feeling of being out of touch—

mannequins attempting empathy,
looking out over great distances
as flesh turns stone into different

kinds of music. Competing against
notions of coterie, I wonder
if the mind's soft boundaries allow

for sense-extensions between me
and those appointed men preaching
spirit techniques. I listen to the cello's
earthy sub-tones and try to become

who I was before the District
blinded me when the school
caught fire and trucks in the fields
blasted early Pavement backed by star

martyrs wailing on modified guitars
and sex is what I heard behind
the fireworks stand closing down

the hour I found my future between
where I was and where I'd be the fire part
of fire burning panic off the sheets.

Static

Island Hopping

Kids cut trails between compounds.
Someone smudges a zygote with their heel.

And the music! Margot flashing
Her chest; Jefferson flexing his back.

To possess an interval of life
that isn't his, he tracks faces on screen
until his password into fame
is the trumpet blast of trying to endure
who he's become by adding
to the spectacle as though it is a garden,
and he, a metal ornament flashing in the sun.
The day he says he is a human bomb
he profits many zeroes. Reaching for the Xannie
in his drawer he sees the logo on the carpet
as the negation of the life that sewed it
into place—a fact he keeps inside
till the day he jumps through the floor-
to-ceiling window in his office.

In the city's narrow streets
I pose on my bike as the good doctor
offering jokes to sisters
losing brothers in screens. I pose
as every passing trend,
as meaning living a longer
life in words. I pose as a harlequin
led through the night on a leash by a girl
singing I Am Come America.
I model my death after the dog's.
I pose in photographs, till everything
I've been and everything I'll ever be
is the faceless man standing in the warm
sea, holding up a late Rothko.

Static

Ratio

Near the end, I'm feeling pretty good.
But when the secrets I've traded

Are traded again, I feel like Henry
Kissinger carving people out of wood.

⁘⁘⁘

Because I'm always saying no
to Nebraskans asking favors, when I'm not
studying for tests on East Asia,
I'm hard at work on my translation

of *Meditation at Lagunitas,*
which I'm selling as an app to the top
officials in The United Arab
Emirates, who are inventing strategies

to manage The Great American
Reset, because it's August on this plane,
and I'm wet all over as commercial
pilots toy with something small

and plastic, and their attendants play
dress-up with a less-than-average
class. In pleasure's wide arrangement,

someone's mother is standing, blinking
through the idea of later. Someone
else's mother wears a pair of hotel slippers

against the will of someone else's
mother, whose name I'll never mention.
Drinking bourbon, someone's father
wears a mask and moves his hand

over someone's angry daughter.
Fumbling with strap, he sips from a glass
and tries to deliver a moving sermon,

but he is interrupted by someone eating
dim sum, and someone else supervising
a soft labor outside the neutral zone.

Walking the streets in my winter
coat, I'm counting necks
in the stems of 1950 leaves.
I stop and sit in the sad chair

and become that figure watching
the neo-formalist and language kids
write symphonies outside
O'Brien's apartment in winter

when the songs are male to females
and female to males leaving
the hulls of strange boats to chase

puppets through fields of unmade
music. Inside the startled iris,
I'm rescuing coffin flowers from

the milk sea, whose grid is a burial
ground for those harboring
seed into the new era.
I bury pieces of blue glass in hills

called water as lines of smoke
soften stone and fish observe
the country, the contrails in tide-pools
I push my fingers through.

Easing tensions, hot balloons
make notes inside me before I lose
control and a panic flows so quietly,

it doesn't have a source, like that
dream called 40 Ways to Lose Myself
By Becoming Something Else.

Static

The Triumph of Life

. . . absolute silence is possible only in death.
There is no one to corroborate this.

:::::::

Thinking something romantic about the novel
I'm in this looped recording
trying to describe what I've seen
as lines go down on streets with Spenser
in ergo of Schuyler capturing hymns
in a collage of sacraments. When the crazy in power
produce more than broken radios
out of praise for the archive
I'll leave today alone. If I've missed
my chance to find meaning
and the ocean is really diminishing
along with my faith that someday
I'll repose in its over-described arms
then tonight I'll fall into bed
thinking something romantic about the novel.

NOTES

Some of the language on page 39 and 43 is indebted to Don DeLillo's *Falling Man*, and Bonnie Prince Billy's "You Want That Picture," respectively.

"Triumph of Life" is after Shelley.

ACKNOWLEDGMENTS

Grateful acknowledgement is made to the editors of: *Barn Owl Review, Catch Up, Court Green, Interim, The Laurel Review, New American Writing, Octopus, Omniverse, Slope,* and *Third Coast*, where some of these poems first appeared. Sections of *January Machine* were also published as a chapbook (titled *Bloom*) by *The Laurel Review* / Green Tower Press.

I give my deepest gratitude to Ryan Murphy, Martha Rhodes, and everyone at Four Way Books. For their company and encouragement throughout the writing of this book, I send my love to Crissie McMullan, Jeremy N. Smith, Chris Dombrowski, and Youna Kwak; Amanda Nadelberg, Alan Felsenthal, Melanie Noel, Adam Roberts, Margaret Ross, and Daniel Poppick; Wil and Kisha.

Rob Schlegel is the author of *The Lesser Fields* (Center for Literary Publishing). He serves as co-editor of The Catenary Press, which is dedicated to publishing long poems. His writing has appeared in *Boston Review*, *Columbia Poetry Review*, *Jacket2*, *New American Writing*, *The Volta*, and elsewhere. Born in Portland, Oregon, he has lived most recently in Iowa, Montana, and Washington.